WRESTLING SUPERSTARS

TRIPLE H

By J. R. Kinley

Kaleidoscope
Minneapolis, MN

The Quest for Discovery Never Ends

This edition first published in 2020 by Kaleidoscope Publishing, Inc.

For information regarding permission, write to Kaleidoscope Publishing, Inc.
6012 Blue Circle Drive
Minnetonka, MN 55343

Library of Congress Control Number
2019940205

ISBN
978-1-64519-089-9 (library bound)
978-1-64494-228-4 (paperback)
978-1-64519-192-6 (ebook)

Printed in the United States of America.

Bigfoot lurks within one of the images in this book. It's up to you to find him!

TABLE OF
CONTENTS

CHAPTER 1

Royal Rumble Comeback

Triple H had been down a long road. He tore a leg muscle in 2001. It was a big deal. He was out of the ring for almost a year. Some people might have given up. But Triple H kept training. He wanted to return to wrestling. Royal Rumble 2002 was his chance.

Triple H faced many famous opponents, such as the Undertaker.

Thirty wrestlers compete at Royal Rumble. There are many wrestlers at once. Someone new comes in every ninety seconds. Wrestlers are **eliminated** one by one. The last one standing wins.

Referees would sometimes
yell at Triple H.

The match was underway. Stone Cold Steve Austin had eliminated everyone in the ring. Then the buzzer sounded. The main screen lit the arena. The words *The Game* appeared on the screen. It was one of Triple H's nicknames. The fans cheered. He was back! Rock music played. Triple H entered the ring. He was wearing black. He was ready to fight.

Triple H and Austin locked eyes. They traded punches. More wrestlers entered. One was Kurt Angle. He wore red, white, and blue. People thought he would win. He slammed the other wrestlers around.

FUN FACT
Triple H's first ring name was Terra Ryzing.

Soon, it was down to two. Angle ran at Triple H. But Triple H kicked him in the face. He charged at Angle. Angle threw him to the mat. Triple H charged him again. Angle used a **back body drop**. It sent Triple H over the top rope. Angle put his fists in the air. He thought he won.

But Triple H pulled himself back in. He hit Angle with a clothesline. Angle flew over the top rope. He fell out of the ring. Triple H had done it. He was the last one standing. It was a huge comeback.

Triple H is known as one of the most accomplished wrestlers.

CHAPTER 2

Hunter Hearst Helmsley

Triple H's real name is Paul Levesque (le-VECK). He was born on July 27, 1969. He grew up in New Hampshire. A new gym opened in town when he was a teenager.

He went to check it out. Levesque saw people **bodybuilding**. He thought it was really cool. He started working out. He even won a bodybuilding contest.

To be a successful wrestler, a person needs to be strong.

Levesque met Ted Arcidi. Arcidi was a weightlifter. He was also a pro wrestler. He inspired Levesque. Levesque decided to become a pro wrestler, too. He went to a pro wrestling school. He wrestled in small **promotions**. Then he joined World Championship Wrestling (WCW). But he wanted to wrestle the best. He met with Vince McMahon. McMahon owned World Wrestling Federation (WWF). He offered Levesque a job.

Triple H likes to show off his moves in the ring.

Levesque started with WWF in 1995. He wrestled as Hunter Hearst Helmsley. He tied his long hair back with a ribbon. He wore a fancy white shirt. He was known for dirty tricks.

Helmsley was set to wrestle Mr. Perfect in October 1996. But they got into a fight before the match. Helmsley attacked him. He hurt Perfect's knee. Perfect couldn't wrestle. He convinced Marc Mero to fight in his place. Mero held the Intercontinental Title.

FUN FACT
One of Triple H's nicknames is King of Kings.

It was a heated contest. At one point, Helmsley got a folding chair. He wanted to hit Mero with it. But Mero's wife, Sable, climbed onto the edge of the ring. She grabbed the chair. Then Mr. Perfect entered. He took the chair. Mr. Perfect held it in the air. It looked like he would hit Helmsley with it. The crowd cheered. But he turned. He hit Mero instead! Everyone was shocked. Sable screamed. Mero fell to the mat. Helmsley covered him for the three-count. Helmsley and Mr. Perfect were working together all along. They held the title belt in the air. This was Helmsley's first big title. It was also one of his first big tricks.

BOSS'S DAUGHTER

Triple H is married to Stephanie McMahon. She is Vince McMahon's daughter. Their romance started as a story line. They were just acting. But then it became real. They got married in 2003.

Wrestlers usually stay in character while wrestling.

CHAPTER 3

Triple H

Hunter Hearst Helmsley was a perfect **heel**. But he could do more. Helmsley worked with wrestler Shawn Michaels. They started D-Generation X (DX) in 1997. DX invaded **rival** WCW's headquarters. They wanted to show who ruled pro wrestling. They rode together in a military vehicle. The fans loved it.

Helmsley had changed. There were no more fancy shirts. He was the rebel leader of DX. He went by the name Triple H. He was a skilled leader. Dwayne "the Rock" Johnson led another group. It was called the Nation of Domination. The two groups became rivals.

Judgment Day 2000 was an Iron Man match. Triple H and the Rock would wrestle for one hour. Whoever had the most pins would win. It was heel against **face**.

Triple H tried to intimidate people in the ring.

In 2017, Triple H said he would be willing to wrestle the Rock again.

Lights flashed in the arena. The bell rang. Fans cheered for both wrestlers. The Rock hit his Rock Bottom slam. He scored the first pin.

The Rock got Triple H's leg in a hold. Triple H escaped. But his knee was hurt. The wrestlers faced each other. The Rock crouched low. Triple H set up his signature move. It was called the Pedigree. He reached over the Rock. He hooked his arms around the Rock's elbows. He locked the Rock's arms behind his back. Then he drove him face-first into the mat. The Pedigree took the Rock down for a three-count. Triple H scored his first pin. The battle continued. With only a few minutes left, they were tied 5–5. The crowd roared.

FUN FACT

The Rock said some of his matches with Triple H were the greatest he's ever had.

Triple H's DX friends came into the ring. They took out the Rock. Suddenly, The Undertaker rode in on his motorcycle. The fans went crazy. He attacked everyone. The buzzer rang. The Undertaker and the ref were the only two standing. The ref called a penalty on the Undertaker. Triple H got a penalty point. The air filled with boos and cheers. Triple H claimed the WWF Championship.

Triple H has won many championships.

THE
PEDIGREE

Hooks arms under opponent's arms

Jumps up

Slams opponent to mat

CHAPTER 4

Triple H sometimes used a hammer as a prop while wrestling.

King of Kings

Triple H's career changed when he was in his forties. He got what he called a "real job." World Wrestling Entertainment (WWE) made him Chief Operating Officer. Later, he became an executive vice president. He helps develop new talent. His experience in the ring helps him lead others. And he still wrestles.

Triple H went to Royal Rumble 2016. It was a title match. The winner of Royal Rumble would be WWE World Heavyweight Champion.

FUN FACT

In the early 2000s, WWF changed its name to World Wrestling Entertainment (WWE).

The buzzer sounded. Triple H entered the arena. He was the last one to enter the ring. The fans cheered. They were excited to see the legend back. Six wrestlers remained. Roman Reigns was the only one standing up.

Triple H and Reigns stared each other down. They punched each other. The other wrestlers joined in. Soon, only four remained. They were Reigns, Triple H, Sheamus, and Dean Ambrose.

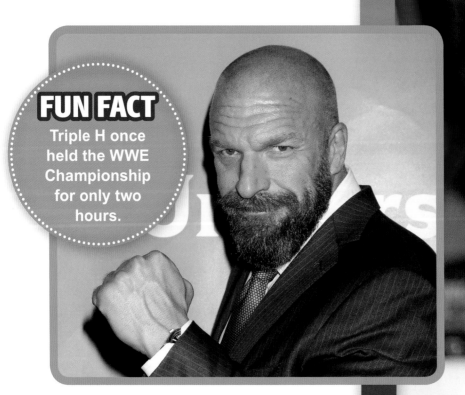

FUN FACT

Triple H once held the WWE Championship for only two hours.

Triple H has his own action figure.

CAREER HIGHLIGHTS

1995

1995
Paul Levesque debuts with WWF as Hunter Hearst Helmsley.

1996

1996
Triple H wins his first WWF Intercontinental Championship. He'll go on to win it four more times.

1997
Triple H wins his first of two European Championships.

1997

1997
Triple H wins King of the Ring.

1999

1999
Triple H wins his first WWE Championship Title.

2001
Triple H wins his first of three Tag Team Championships.

2001

2002
Triple H makes a comeback by winning Royal Rumble after a major injury.

2002

2002
Triple H wins his first World Heavyweight Championship. He'll go on to win it four more times.

2011
Triple H starts working as WWE Chief Operating Officer.

2011

2016
Triple H wins Royal Rumble.

2016

The wrestlers battled fiercely. Triple H and Ambrose were the last ones left. Only one could win. Ambrose threw crazy flying fists at Triple H. Then Ambrose nearly threw him over the top rope. Triple H hung on. Ambrose tried to push him to the floor. But Triple H leaned through the ropes. He got Ambrose onto his shoulders. Then he flipped him overhead. Ambrose landed on the floor. The bell rang. Triple H had won his second Royal Rumble. And he claimed the WWE Championship.

Triple H has won fourteen WWE World Championships. He's had an amazing career. He may have a "real job" now. But he keeps wrestling. And he keeps winning. He's still the King of Kings.

In 2019, Triple H, center, continued to participate in the WWE.

THE BOOK

After reading the book, it's time to think about what you learned.
Try the following exercises to jumpstart your ideas.

THINK

DIFFERENT SOURCES. Consider what types of sources you might be able to find about Triple H. How could each source be useful in its own way?

CREATE

PRIMARY SOURCES. A primary source provides a firsthand account of an event. Some examples of primary sources include interviews, videos, and photographs. Create a list of the types of primary sources that you might be able to find on Triple H.

SHARE

WHAT'S YOUR OPINION? John Cena said Triple H is one of the best competitors to ever step in the ring. Do you agree with this? Find evidence from the book that supports your opinion. Share your opinion and evidence with a friend. Does your friend find your argument convincing?

GROW

DRAWING CONNECTIONS. The text states that Triple H has helped develop pro wrestling talent. How is this important to professional wrestling? Draw a diagram that shows how new talent relates to professional wrestling. How does understanding talent development help you to better understand professional wrestling?

RESEARCH NINJA

Visit *www.ninjaresearcher.com/0899* to learn how
to take your research skills and book report writing to the next level!

RESEARCH

**DIGITAL
LITERACY
TOOLS**

SEARCH LIKE A PRO
Learn about how to use search
engines to find useful websites.

FACT OR FAKE?
Discover how you can tell
a trusted website from an
untrustworthy resource.

TEXT DETECTIVE
Explore how to zero in
on the information you
need most.

SHOW YOUR WORK
Research responsibly—
learn how to cite sources.

WRITE

GET TO THE POINT
Learn how to express
your main ideas.

PLAN OF ATTACK
Learn prewriting exercises
and create an outline.

**DOWNLOADABLE
REPORT
FORMS**

29

Further Resources

BOOKS

Scheff, Matt. *Triple H*. Abdo, 2014.

Shields, Brian. *Triple H*. DK, 2009.

Stone, Adam. *Triple H*. Bellwether Media, 2012.

WEBSITES

FACTSURFER

Factsurfer.com gives you a safe, fun way to find more information.

1. Go to www.factsurfer.com.

2. Enter "Triple H" into the search box and click 🔍.

3. Select your book cover to see a list of related websites.

Glossary

back body drop: A back body drop is when a wrestler bends forward, lifts the opponent overhead, and throws the opponent behind his back. When Triple H charged Angle, Angle used a back body drop to send him over the ropes.

bodybuilding: Bodybuilding is developing and strengthening the body's muscles through exercise, lifting weights, and nutrition. Triple H entered bodybuilding competitions.

eliminated: To be eliminated is to be removed or taken out. Wrestlers are eliminated from the Royal Rumble when they go over the top rope and both feet touch the floor.

face: Short for *babyface*, a face is a wrestler who is a heroic fan favorite. The fans cheered for the face and booed the heel.

heel: A pro wrestling heel is a wrestler who is viewed as a bad guy and hated by fans. Triple H had many fans even though he was a heel.

promotions: Promotions are pro wrestling organizations or companies that plan and put on wrestling events. Triple H got his start wrestling in small promotions.

rival: A rival is an equally matched opponent or enemy. Triple H and the Rock led rival groups.

Index

PHOTO CREDITS

ABOUT THE AUTHOR

J. R. Kinley is a writer and artist. She is part of a wrestling family from Ohio in one of the top wrestling regions in the nation. Her husband, Shaun Kinley, former NCAA wrestler at The Ohio State University, coaches at the nationally ranked St. Edward High School. Together, they operate Kinley Studio.